Stratford Library Association
2203 Main Street
Stratford, CT 06615
203-385-4160

Y0-BZL-062

LATINOS
IN THE
LIMELIGHT

Christina Aguilera

Antonio Banderas

Jeff Bezos

Oscar De La Hoya

Cameron Díaz

Jennifer Lopez

Ricky Martin

Selena

CHELSEA HOUSE PUBLISHERS

LATINOS
IN THE
LIMELIGHT

Jeff Bezos

Virginia Brackett

CHELSEA HOUSE PUBLISHERS
Philadelphia

Frontis: *His revolutionary approach to the potential of the Internet makes Amazon.com founder Jeff Bezos a man who commands the respect of his peers.*

Produced by
21st Century Publishing and Communications, Inc.
New York, New York
http://www.21cpc.com

CHELSEA HOUSE PUBLISHERS

Editor in Chief: Sally Cheney
Production Manager: Pamela Loos
Art Director: Sara Davis
Director of Photography: Judy L. Hasday
Managing Editor: James D. Gallagher
Senior Production Editor: J. Christopher Higgins
Publishing Coordinator: James McAvoy
Project Editor: Anne Hill

The Chelsea House World Wide Web address is
http://www.chelseahouse.com

First Printing

1 3 5 7 9 8 6 4 2

Library of Congress Cataloging-in-Publication Data

Brackett, Virginia.
    Jeff Bezos / Virginia Brackett.
        p. cm. – (Latinos in the limelight)
    Includes bibliographical references (p.) and index.
    ISBN 0-7910-6104-3 (hardcover) — ISBN 0-7910-6105-1 (pbk.)
        1. Bezos, Jeffrey—Juvenile literature 2. Amazon.com—History—Juvenile
    literature. 3. Internet bookstores—United States—Juvenile literature.
    4. Electronic commerce—United States—Juvenile literature. [1. Bezos, Jeffrey.
    2. Booksellers and bookselling. 3. Businesspeople. 4. Hispanic Americans—
    Biography. 5. Amazon.com.] I. Title. II. Series.

    Z473.B47 B73 2000
    380.1'45002'02854678—dc21

                                                                    00—060003
                                                                         CIP
                                                                          AC

CONTENTS

TIME

PERSON OF THE YEAR

AMAZON.COM'S
JEFF BEZOS

E-COMMERCE IS
CHANGING THE WAY
THE WORLD SHOPS

A MAN WHOSE
TIME HAD COME

In December 1999, fans of *Time* magazine anxiously awaited an announcement. Each year since 1927, *Time* has chosen a "Person of the Year" to appear on its cover and to feature in its main article. The magazine's editors select the individual whom they believe has had the greatest influence over events in the past year, whether that influence be good or bad.

Many U.S. presidents, including Franklin D. Roosevelt, Harry Truman, Dwight D. Eisenhower, Richard Nixon, Jimmy Carter, George Bush, and Ronald Reagan, have appeared on the magazine's cover, as have such world leaders as Germany's Adolph Hitler, France's Charles DeGaulle, and the U.S.S.R.'s Nikita Khrushchev. Groups, such as American Apollo 8 astronauts, William Anders, Frank Borman, and Jim Lovell and American women in general, have also been seen on this important magazine cover. So much anticipation exists over the new choice each year that in 1999, *Time* conducted a poll on the Internet, allowing members of the public to vote for their own favorite candidates.

When Jeff Bezos was named Time *magazine's Person of the Year in 1999, he became a member of a very exclusive group of people. The choice signaled just how influential both the Internet and e-commerce had become.*

But that year a different type of individual appeared on the cover of *Time*. The Person of the Year was Jeff Bezos, chief executive officer (CEO) and founder of Amazon.com, a wildly successful business that conducts sales strictly over the Internet. Jeff Bezos's company began selling books exclusively in 1995. By 1999 the company had expanded to include an extremely wide range of products and services. It even began offering its customers the chance to bid on various items in an Internet auction and to shop at many other online "store fronts." Truly Jeff Bezos, the adopted son of a Cuban refugee, represented a man of his time. Only a decade before, Internet businesspeople like Jeff did not exist.

Before companies like Amazon.com could conduct business through Internet-linked computers, the World Wide Web had to be created. Technicians first began to electronically link computers in the 1960s, when the U.S. Department of Defense saw communications between computers as important to the protection of the country.

A few individuals purchased their own personal computers in the 1970s, a time when Jeff was still in grade school. But the technology and language codes needed to link those home computers to one another did not appear until almost 20 years later.

At first, computers hooked to one another through systems called Local Area Networks, or LANs. Big businesses and universities took advantage of LANs to exchange information regarding research, business, and finance. Before personal computers used in individual homes could connect to the network, which was later called the Internet, better security and privacy systems had to be developed. Otherwise, certain computer-literate people, called hackers, could intentionally enter anyone's computer and read or even destroy information stored there.

By 1990, many of these problems were overcome, and more than 300,000 computers were hooked together through networks. However, the greatest growth in the Internet would not occur for a few more years.

Jeff was able to become an important Internet figure, because by the mid-1990s, millions of people had started using this complex network of computers, which had spread over almost every country in the world. Any individual could exchange messages with any other individual through E-mail (the "e" meaning "electronic"). No longer did people necessarily require telephones or envelopes and stamps to communicate. They could do so by typing in messages on a keyboard; moments later the message could be read by someone on the other side of the world courtesy of technology.

Once these developments had taken place and the framework had been established, Jeff Bezos could conceive of an electronic store named Amazon.com. "He has helped guarantee that the world of buying and selling will never be the same," editor James Kelly wrote about Jeff in *Time* magazine's 1999 Person of the Year issue.

At age 35, Jeff's selection as Person of the Year made him the fourth-youngest individual to receive this prestigious title. The only people younger than Jeff to be chosen were 25-year-old American aviator Charles A. Lindbergh (1927); 26-year-old Queen

Elizabeth II of England (1952); and 34-year-old American civil rights leader Martin Luther King Jr. (1963).

While at 35, Jeff seemed young to be chosen for the honor, he had been an incredibly youthful 31 when, in 1995, he acted on his vision to form an Internet store named after the world's second longest river, the Amazon.

Jeff knew he had a great idea when he first developed his Internet site to engage in what some call "e-commerce" or "e-tailing," instead of retailing. While it began as a place to buy books, by 1999 Amazon.com offered a number of other products as well.

When asked why he chose books as his main product, Jeff explained that people buy books for two reasons. They "need" books, and they find books "fun." He liked the idea of combining necessity with pleasure.

An important aspect of Amazon.com is its ability to offer items at discount prices. That's because Jeff does not have to buy or rent a retail space for customers to visit in order to do business, so he saves on the expenses such buildings bring, referred to as "overhead." Although he could pocket those savings himself, he believes in sharing his good fortune with his customers by offering them lower prices. And by doing so, he knowingly attracts more people to buy from him.

The customer is all-important to Jeff. He has said that if his business does a good job, customers will spread the word. And indeed they have. According to one writer, "Since its debut on the World Wide Web in July 1995, Amazon.com has become the model to watch and to envy." Back in 1995 when Jeff first started his business, he asked 300 family members and friends to tell others about his website. He did not advertise at all for the first 30 days and still sold books in all 50 states within the United States and in 45 countries around the world.

Now any Internet user can easily find Amazon.com by entering that name into the address field of a computer homepage that can perform a search for Internet sites. Immediately a dazzling array of choices appears on the screen. A group of tabs across the top of the page bear different labels and wait to be chosen by a click of the mouse: Books; DVD & Video; Electronics & Software; Toys & Video Games are just a few.

When customers find an item they want, they can click a button that allows them to add it to their "shopping basket" until they're ready to "check out." By using terms such as these that are already familiar to shoppers, Jeff knows he can make his customers feel comfortable during their online shopping experience. When his customer is ready to order, an easy-to-use screen appears, requesting information necessary for payment and shipping. One reporter wrote, "You want a book? You browse, you point, you click, you pay, you read." Amazon.com further developed its so-called "one-click" technology, which can store billing and shipping information securely, so that returning customers don't have to reenter the data each time they shop. The company started to use this technology online in September 1997.

This technology was so innovative that Amazon.com filed for a patent to protect it from being copied by competitors without Amazon.com's permission and was granted a patent in September 1999. Just a few weeks later, the company filed a lawsuit against bn.com, another online venture set up in May 1997 by Barnes & Noble, a New York-based bookstore chain. Amazon.com charged its online bookselling rival with copying Amazon.com's "one-click" technology. In the end, bn.com was not allowed to use Amazon.com's one-click technology, and soon after they launched a new system which they called "express checkout."

Amazon's Internet commerce had become a big business that needed protecting. While Jeff does not release his sales figures, he did say in 1997 that the company was growing at a whopping rate of 3,000 percent each year!

Part of Jeff's success is his ability to include the customer in the buying process in ways

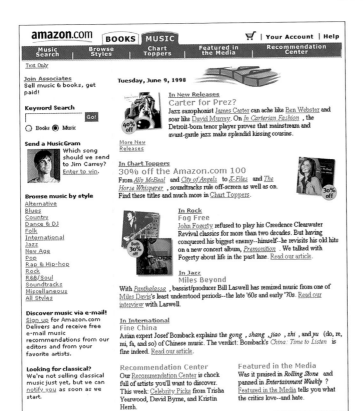

In 1998, Amazon.com added music to its growing list of items for sale, providing a much greater selection than any traditional store. In the same year, Amazon.com opened sites in the United Kingdom and Germany.

other than just as a shopper. He doesn't simply sell the books to customers. He also lets readers write to Amazon.com to tell what they think about the books. Then the company posts that message as a book review. That way, a fan of Harry Potter who lives in Colorado can find out what a reader in South Carolina thinks about the latest Potter adventure. This also allows customers to learn ahead of time what kind of product they are buying.

Jeff explained, "With most products the price of the product is only the beginning of what you pay. With a book, $25 is less important than the eight hours you spend with it." When he was asked if he'd worry that a reader might be discouraged about purchasing a book that had received a bad review, Jeff said no. He explained, "If you have a limited selection, then you have to try and sell people what you have. If you have an unlimited selection, you can sell them what's right for them."

His approach must be working well. One 1999 survey showed that more than half of American adults know the name Amazon.com, an incredible statistic for a business that doesn't own one store in any mall.

Amazingly, for a business that has so many customers, Amazon.com has not yet shown a profit. It has never made more money than it spends on the business itself. Rather than paying money to his investors—those who buy stock in Amazon.com in order to own part of the company—Jeff instead uses the income to pay more employee salaries, to build more warehouses to store his products, and to make business partnerships with other companies.

The fact that the company has yet to make a profit doesn't seem to bother its investors. Many who bought the company stock in its first two years were wealthy in 1999, when the price per share had increased many times over. With all of their valuable stock, shareholders seem content to wait until 2001, the year in which Jeff predicts that the company will make a profit.

If anyone can do it, Jeff can. Those who know him say that Jeff seems always in control. A simple man, he continued to drive a Honda Accord and share a small Seattle apartment with his wife, MacKenzie, long after his personal worth equaled millions of dollars. They didn't move into a house until late in 1999, as they anticipated the birth of their first child the following March.

Jeff inspires his employees, many of whom have a strong loyalty to the company. During his first visit to a new company warehouse in Kansas, the 300 new employees there told him that they had heard rumors that Amazon was going to fail. Jeff answered honestly that he doesn't worry about such predictions. He explained that he did not feel the need to convince his critics that Amazon is a good deal. He just wants to convince his customers. When the question-and-answer period between Jeff and his employees ended, many of the workers asked Jeff to autograph whatever they had handy, from hard hats to dollar bills. They must have believed the company was not only not going to fail, but was going to be a great success.

In 1999, Jeff Bezos, posing here with Sotheby's President Diane D. Brooks, continued to expand Amazon.com by forming strategic alliances. Amazon.com's deal with Sotheby's allowed the site to offer its customers online auctions.

One of the gifted people Jeff lured to Amazon.com is Joseph Galli, above, formerly an executive at Black & Decker.

Jeff has been able to tempt top executives away from comfortable positions at companies such as the small appliance and tool maker Black & Decker and the huge retailer Sears, once the country's most successful store. Some say people can't resist Jeff's hearty infectious laugh.

Jeff's supporters attribute his ability to captivate others to his gung-ho enthusiasm. During the 1998 Christmas season, that same enthusiasm motivated Jeff to join his warehouse employees on the work floor. He helped them pack customer books, toys, and other items when Amazon was swamped with holiday orders. Although his critics called it a publicity stunt, Jeff's action created an unusual image that impressed many. Few wealthy executives have ever been seen rolling up their sleeves and stepping on to their company's production line.

Whatever the cause of his success, Jeff Bezos intends to keep his appointment with a destiny tied to the fate of his company. Perhaps like his grandfather before him, Jeff was meant to explore new frontiers. But as a child growing up near San Antonio, Texas, he could never have anticipated such a future.

2

A New Family,
A New Future

Born January 12, 1964, in New Mexico, Jeffrey Preston spent much of his early years in Cotulla, Texas, a small town in the southern part of the state. His mother, Jaklyn "Jackie" Gise, traces her family lines to the early 1800s in America. Jackie's ancestor Colonel Robert Hall moved from Tennessee to San Antonio, Texas. In an ancient-looking photograph that hung in Jeff's home, Colonel Hall looked as if he deserved his reputation as a colorful character. He dressed for the photo in a strange outfit consisting of various stitched-together animal pelts. At 6' 4", Colonel Hall presented a striking figure. Jeff's mother has said that when the colonel strolled through San Antonio, "the crowds would part."

Jackie's great-grandfather Bernhardt Vesper was responsible for the family's location in Cotulla, Texas. He purchased a 25,000-acre ranch, called the LAZY G Ranch, that has remained in the family ever since.

Jackie's father and Jeff's beloved grandfather, Lawrence Preston "Pop" Gise, lived for a time in Albuquerque, New Mexico. He spent his entire working

This 1970 photo shows an Amtrack train crossing Central Avenue in downtown Albuquerque, New Mexico, on its trip from Los Angeles, California to Chicago, Illinois. Jeff's father and grandfather lived in Albuquerque for a while.

career in a government position as head of the former Atomic Energy Commission. The region he supervised included seven southwestern states. Pop retired at a young age and moved his family back to the Texas ranch.

As a boy, Jeff spent many happy summers there with his grandparents. His grandmother, Mattie Louis Strait, was a relative of the popular country singer George Strait. Jeff found a freedom on the ranch with his grandparents that he would recall fondly when he became an adult.

Like the adults before her, Jackie had a strong independent spirit. A headstrong teen when she married, Jackie had her first child, Jeff, when she was just 17 years old. Her young marriage ended after only a year, when Jeff's father left the family. Jeff has no memories of his biological father.

When Jeff was four years old, his mother married again, this time to a man named Miguel "Mike" Bezos. Mike shared the pioneering spirit of Jackie's family. In the 1960s, at the young age of 15, Mike left his home in Cuba and relocated to the United States. A Roman Catholic mission offered Mike a temporary home, a great relief to a teenager who owned only a single shirt in addition to the clothes he was wearing. Bright and anxious to learn, Mike studied hard to acquire English as his second language. After working at a number of odd jobs, he managed to gain admission to the University of Albuquerque.

During his stint as a late shift employee at a bank, Mike met Jackie, who also worked there. They fell in love and married, giving Jeff the only father he has ever known. The bond that formed between Mike and Jeff was so strong that Jeff had no desire to learn anything about his birth father. "I've never been curious about him," Jeff has said. "The only time it comes up is in the doctor's office when I'm asked for my medical history. I put down that I just don't know." With obvious pride, he added, "My real father is the guy who raised me."

Mike Bezos officially adopted Jeff, who in turn chose to adopt Mike's Cuban heritage. This closeness has caused some reports to mistakenly identify Mike as Jeff's birth father.

Mike finished his studies to become a petroleum engineer, someone who helps locate fossil fuels such as oil. His training allowed him to take a job with the large oil company Exxon, and over the next few years, the family lived in Houston and Miami. He later became an Exxon executive in a management position. A self-made man in every sense of the word, Mike Bezos acted as an excellent example for his high-achieving, adopted son.

Like any family, the Bezos household has its stories to tell about the children. One of the best-known stories about Jeff focuses on an incident that took place when he was just a toddler. Reportedly, he asked his mother to allow him to move from his baby bed to an adult bed. Not yet ready to allow her young son to make that change, Jackie said no. Showing the intelligence and motivation that would prove crucial later in his life, Jeff decided to act on his own, without his mother's help. The young boy found a screwdriver and patiently worked on his crib until it lay in pieces on the floor. That early act indicated that the Bezos family could look forward to the unexpected from their eldest child.

When Jeff was six years old, his baby sister, Christina, was born. A year later, brother Mark

Jeff's adoptive father, Mike, built a successful career at Exxon Oil, working at an oil refinery much like the one pictured here. Jeff adopted Mike's Cuban heritage and said of him, "My real father is the guy who raised me."

joined the growing family. Although as adults the brothers and sister remain close, they suffered the normal sibling arguments while growing up. When his younger sister and brother tried to enter his room, Jeff immediately put a stop to the invasion. He set up a buzzer that acted like a burglar alarm, sounding a warning if anyone tried to push through the door. His fascination with tinkering grew as he assembled models and worked with a Radio Shack electronics kit, a gift from Pop.

Enthralled in grade school with the Infinity Cube, a gadget using motorized mirrors that allowed the user to stare into "infinity," the boy asked for a cube as a gift. Because the family could not afford its $20 price tag, Jeff bought some inexpensive materials and made his own cube. This story about Jeff was later included in *Turning on Bright Minds: A Parent Looks at Gifted Education in Texas*, a book published in the Houston area in the 1970s.

Clearly inventive, Jeff acted upon his instinct for gadgets as he matured. By the time he was 14 years old, he wanted to become an astronaut or study physics. His family later came up with a name for Jeff's experimental years—the "solar-cooker era." The name came from a solar oven powered by the sun that Jeff created from an umbrella and aluminum foil. The family garage became his laboratory and the site of several experiments. On one occasion, the teenager used a vacuum cleaner to try to concoct a hover craft, a machine that floats above the ground on air.

During summers spent at his grandparents' ranch in Texas, Jeff put his mechanical skills to good use. Pop taught him to repair machinery, such as tractors and windmills. Never shy about discussing time spent on the ranch, Jeff eagerly tells how he and Pop managed to repair a D6 Caterpillar tractor by reading instructions from a stack of manuals 3 feet tall. By the time he was 16, Jeff could lay pipe and use an arc welder. He also rode horses, worked cattle like a pro, and helped Pop brand his calves. He learned a valuable life skill on the LAZY G Ranch: patience. According to Jeff, that's something one needs a lot of "on a ranch in the middle of nowhere."

In school, Jeff had a clean-cut image. He was well liked in spite of the fact that he didn't drink alcohol, do drugs, or use curse words. Jeff became class president. Later he was valedictorian, the top student, at Palmetto High School in Miami. In addition to Mike Bezos, Jeff's role models included Thomas Edison, the great American inventor, and Walt Disney, founder of the Disney entertainment empire. However, the Disney movies did not impress Jeff as much as the theme parks did. He enjoyed Disney World so much that he returned to visit six times.

As an adult, Jeff labeled Walt Disney's vision "powerful." He talked about Walt Disney with great respect, saying, "He knew exactly what he wanted to build and teamed up with a bunch of really smart people and built it. Everyone thought it wouldn't work, and he had to persuade the banks to lend him $400 million. But he did it." Most of those words would also describe Jeff himself when he set about to invent an online store while in his early 30s.

Before his career began, Jeff got a rigorous education at Princeton University in New Jersey. Thinking he would follow Pop in the field of physics, Jeff first chose that subject as his major. But like many college students, he decided during his second year to change his plans. With electrical engineering and computer science as his major, Jeff graduated summa cum laude, with highest honors. He received his bachelor's degree in 1986.

The graduate's first job was with a company named Fitel. A brand new group, Fitel worked to link people in various jobs who could help handle worldwide financial trades. As a young man with much promise, Jeff didn't stay long in his first position. After about two years at

Fitel, he went to work for Bankers Trust, another company with interest in financial dealings. Following two years at his second job, Jeff landed an interview with a new company called D. E. Shaw.

Most companies have set tasks in mind that they want their employees to complete. They develop job descriptions, then hire qualified people. D. E. Shaw reversed that approach. Its executives searched out intelligent people, then matched those people to specific tasks.

David Shaw, the founder of the company, had a background in college teaching, having taught computer science at Columbia University in New York City. Shaw had been convinced to move into the business world by an executive at the Morgan Stanley Company. He had worked on Wall Street for a time, using computers as a tool to identify changes over time in financial markets. By 1988, Shaw was ready to start his own financial business, but he decided to branch out into other areas of interest as well, and his company began to grow.

After interviewing Jeff, one of Shaw's partners told the boss that Jeff would "make someone a lot of money someday." The boss met Jeff, agreed with his partner, and hired the young man. He described Jeff as having an unusual balance between intellect and creativity. He also appreciated Jeff's friendly and enthusiastic personality.

Jeff liked his job at D. E. Shaw for both professional and personal reasons. He soon fell in love with a co-worker named MacKenzie, who worked in the research department. MacKenzie was six years younger than Jeff; like him, she had graduated from Princeton. Hoping to become a novelist, MacKenzie had served as an assistant to the award-winning author Toni Morrison before joining the D. E. Shaw staff. Jeff and MacKenzie dated for a while, and then the couple got married in 1993.

As the years passed, Jeff became a researcher. He first specialized in the insurance business, then computer software, and finally the Internet. He sensed that the Internet would offer huge opportunities but didn't know how to take advantage of them yet. Until 1994, the Internet was mainly used by the Department of Defense. That year the government decided to step out of the Internet and let private business develop it for commercial purposes. As Jeff continued his research, he discovered an incredible figure; According to one source, since the Internet had been opened up for commerce, it was growing at a rate of 2,300 percent each year. Stunned, Jeff considered that figure. He brainstormed for an idea that would allow him to put this incredible instrument to work to his advantage. He later labeled this moment "a wake-up call."

Jeff knew that he should be able to come up with a great idea. After all, thinking was his job. He decided that the Internet could be used to sell products, just as companies did by taking orders over the phone and then shipping the goods to their buyers. But the Internet differed greatly from any sales environment that Jeff had ever known. What product should he sell? Would things that sold well through catalogs sell as well online? And how could he possibly begin a business?

He had the talent and the enthusiasm to engage in an Internet business start-up, but he had no specific experience in sales. More

Jeff's success has made him a popular speaker. Addressing the audience at one conference, Jeff recalls how he transformed his early vision of using the Internet for business into a reality with his online company, Amazon.com.

importantly, he had little money to invest. In order to find answers to these questions, Jeff did what he had always done. He used his imagination and then went to the source he had always trusted for support—his family.

3

A BIG RIVER,
A BIG STORE

Before leaving his comfortable and profitable job at D. E. Shaw as the company's youngest senior vice president to begin an Internet business, Jeff discussed the entire matter with MacKenzie. He didn't go to his wife with some vague idea. Jeff had already been hard at work on a plan to make his vision become a reality. Tremendously excited, he sized up this opportunity, deciding he simply could not be left out of what he knew would be an Internet explosion. He not only wanted to join in, he wanted to serve as a pioneer in electronic commerce. That challenge, more than the chance of making great amounts of money, enticed Jeff. As he would later tell a reporter, he sat in his office thinking, "We can be a complete first mover in e-commerce."

Jeff put his business experience to work, learning everything he could about mail-order companies. He worked with the belief that what sold well by mail could also sell by Internet. A list of the top 20 companies that sold items by mail became his study guide.

His next thought was focused on how he could create,

Jeff speaks at the 2000 American Booksellers Association convention in Chicago. His first visit to an ABA convention in 1994 convinced him that going online would allow him to create a bookstore bigger than any traditional outlet.

in his words, "the most value for customers." This would set a pattern for all of Jeff's future decisions in regards to his company. Customer value must come first. That value could lie in a great selection of products, reduced prices, or in the easy manner by which they could complete their purchases. After all, Jeff has said, "Unless you could create something with a huge value proposition for the customer, it would be easier for them to do it the old way."

There was nothing old about the Internet. Just the new format and the new experience could prove to be valuable. Jeff had to establish his business by using all of the Internet's advantages. The more he considered this, the more appealing the idea of selling books became. Even though many "brick and mortar" bookstores, some of them quite large, already existed, they couldn't begin to hold every book in print. And although books were sold through catalogs, those catalogs couldn't possibly list the millions of titles that existed. The Internet, on the other hand, is based on the computer's capacity to store and reference huge amounts of information. The computer-based business could store billions of digital files, records, and blocks of information.

So, after much consideration, Jeff decided to sell books through his new business. Only one small problem existed—he knew nothing about the book business. Ever ready to tackle a new challenge, Jeff determined to learn as much as he could in as little time as possible. Luckily, the yearly convention of the American Booksellers Association would take place that week in Los Angeles. Jeff booked a flight, jumped on a jet, and flew cross country to visit the convention over a weekend.

In the convention center, merchants set up booths to display the books their companies sell. The booths were organized in long rows in a huge open convention area. They were bordered by curtains and colorful signs and banners that identified the business that occupied the booth. The booths were staffed by eager sales representatives who offered to show their products to passersby.

If anyone had been observing Jeff during those two days, that person would have seen an eager young man strolling up and down each aisle. In a short time, Jeff gathered a huge amount of information. He could find brochures about each business and lists of the books that each one sold, complete with price lists and ordering information.

Jeff did not keep his plans to himself. He approached two of the biggest book whole-salers—groups that sell books to stores, which in turn sell them to the public. Several company representatives for Ingram and for Baker & Tayler listened closely as Jeff explained his plan. To Jeff's delight, he discovered that the book industry had already developed one of the largest data bases, or lists, of any product. The book wholesalers had long lists of books for sale already established on CD-ROM disks.

Fate seemed to have brought Jeff to the convention. All of the information he needed already existed in an organized way that he could use. It was ready to go online. He told one reporter, "There are three million titles in print . . . and with that many titles you can offer something online that you could never offer in a physical store."

When he flew back home at the end of the weekend, Jeff had worked his plan out in his head. He explained to MacKenzie that, in his opinion, books were the best product to sell through the Internet. An intelligent and important member of their team, MacKenzie matched Jeff's enthusiasm with her own. The idea of an adventure appealed to her pioneering spirit. Now they needed to quit their jobs at D. E. Shaw and spend some serious moments considering two frightening barriers to reaching their goals—risk and capital.

When Jeff explained to David Shaw his desire to begin his project, the boss understood. He recognized in Jeff his own desire to accomplish things yet untried. Still, he was not happy to be losing such an extraordinary talent, much less two great employees. He was also concerned about Jeff's future. He suggested that Jeff and MacKenzie spend a few more weeks thinking about their plans before leaving the firm.

Jeff followed his boss's advice. He played a game with himself that he called "regret-minimization framework." That meant that he would think of the best way to make his regrets in life very small. In this game, Jeff imagined himself 50 years later, at age 80, an old man with many years of experiences behind him. He asked his "old man" self whether he would regret losing years of huge Christmas bonuses from D. E. Shaw. He also asked that future Jeff whether he would feel ashamed if his online business had failed.

The answer to both of these questions was no. As Jeff said later, "In fact, I'd have been proud of that, proud of myself for having taken that risk." He knew that he would be especially proud of having participated "in that thing called the Internet." Showing his connection to

the pioneering spirit that his own ancestors and his adoptive father stood for, he added, "It was like the wild, wild West, a new frontier." The only regrets he would have would be if he did not go on this challenging journey.

Then he applied logic to his plans. According to his figures, an Internet business had only a 10 percent chance of succeeding, let alone of making the big mark on the world that Jeff envisioned. Because of his excellent record in reaching his goals, Jeff gave himself three times those chances—a 30 percent chance to succeed. He actually found the idea that he would likely fail liberating. It freed him from the pressure of having to score a huge hit. He told those who

While some people are intimidated by computers, Jeff sees them more as a doorway to tremendous opportunities. He truly relishes the challenging journey his growing online business brings.

would contribute money toward his project, "I think there's a 70% chance you're going to lose all your money, so don't invest unless you can afford to lose."

That prediction might have caused many people to reject Jeff's invitation to invest in his new idea. But those investors were his friends and, more importantly, his family. Mike Bezos recalled the day that he and Jackie heard about Jeff's plans. He, like most Americans at that time, didn't even know what the Internet was. He wondered for a few moments whether Jeff had carefully considered what this new adventure meant for him and MacKenzie.

However, Mike and Jackie did not have to think too long about whether to offer their money. The truth was, they didn't care what kind of business Jeff planned. According to Jackie, she and Mike "talked about it for two minutes" before they pledged the huge sum of $300,000. That money had been set aside for their retirement, but they believed enough in Jeff's ability to risk their own futures. As Jackie explained later, "We didn't invest in Amazon, we invested in Jeff." Their stake in the company allowed them to own 6 percent of Amazon.com, making them billionaires just a few short years later.

On July 4, 1994, Jeff and MacKenzie bid good-bye to his parents. What happened next has become a well-known tale from Internet history. Borrowing Mike Bezos's old Chevy Blazer, the couple left Fort Worth, Texas, and drove all the way to Seattle. Jeff had chosen to start up his business in Seattle for a couple reasons. It served as home for a large number of computer experts, or "tekkies." Also, in nearby Oregon sat a huge book warehouse

belonging to one of the country's biggest distributors, Ingram Book Group. Jeff rented a
two-bedroom home in the Seattle suburb of
Bellevue. With the $1 million borrowed from
family members and friends, Jeff went to work
in a space familiar to him since his child-
hood—the garage.

Always one to save money, Jeff bought
wooden doors and brackets at Home Depot to
construct desks. He used the door-as-desk
plan again a few years later. All of Amazon.com's

*Seattle, Washington,
became the home for
Amazon.com in part
because so many
computer experts live
in the area.*

employees would have desks fashioned from doors. Three computer stations were established in the garage office, and five crew members joined Jeff. They moved back and forth from station to station, avoiding the sea of extension cords that ran from outlets in the house.

The work space sported a large hole in the ceiling which was left from a potbellied stove that had to be pulled out of the garage to make more room. MacKenzie worked part-time with Jeff, performing accounting jobs and interviewing prospective employees. Rumor had it that some of those interviews took place right in the midst of a rival bookseller's store.

Jeff and his employees worked in the garage for the next year. They wanted to produce an Internet site that not only would offer lots of book titles but also would make finding and choosing those titles simple. During that time, Jeff debated about what to call his new enterprise. His first thought was "Cadabra," a shortened form of the magical command "Abracadabra" made famous in Disney movies.

When Jeff asked people what they thought of the name, one person said that the name sounded like "Cadaver," a term that refers to a dead body, and asked "Why would you want to call your company that?" Obviously, the name choice needed more consideration. Jeff later chose the name of the world's second longest river, the Amazon, and Amazon.com was born.

Jeff, MacKenzie, and his crew launched the first version of the company's website in June 1995. A very early form of the site appeared at an address that no longer exists: www.amazon.com:99. A group of about 300

amazon.com.

1 9 9 5	1 9 9 6	1 9 9 7	1 9 9 8	1 9 9 9	2 0 0 0
July Amazon.com opens for business. **October** First 100-order day. First 100-order hour comes less than a year later. 100-order minutes are common today. **September** Seattle Yellow Pages listing under "book-stores" results in customers trying to place orders by phone. We were kind of hoping they'd use the Web site. We don't renew the listing.	**November** Associates Program launched. First Amazon.com Associate is Pure bred PuppyNet. www.puppynet.com. Most common response in the office: "awww..." (Today, there are more than 470,000 Amazon Associates.)	**May** IPO—Amazon.com appears on the NASDAQ as AMZN **September** 1-Click® shopping introduced. **November** Vice President Al Gore drops by. Works customer service phone queues. Looks spiffy in headset. Doesn't do a bad job, at all.	**February** The little guy gets a leg up as Amazon.com Advantage launches, leveling the playing field for independent publishers. **October** We're international! Amazon.co.uk and Amazon.de open. **November** We're ready for our closeup, Mr. DeMille: Amazon.com's Video & DVD Store opens.	**April** Amazon.com e-cards launches, based on the belief that if cards were free, the world would be a better place. **June** 10 millionth customer served **July** Amazon.com Toys opens for business. Customers' Slinky needs, thankfully, are met. **December** Over 20 million items shipped	**January** Customers smile. smiles back. **April** Customers pamper themselves with the Health & Beauty store thanks to drug-store.com's alliance with Amazon.com. **May** Everything you need to furnish your house is just a click away: the Home Living store at Amazon.com opens, in alliance with living.com.

July 1995 / Books

June 1998 / Music

November 1998 / Video & DVD

March 1999 / Auctions

July 1999 / Toys and Electronics

November 1999 / Tools and Hardware

April 2000 / Lawn & Patio

May 2000 / Kitchen

family members and friends tried the hidden website. David Shaw, Jeff and MacKenzie's former employer, also tried. Upon seeing the site, Shaw commented, "Wow, this is it." He found the site to be simple and user-friendly.

On July 16, Amazon.com opened to the public. Jeff depended simply on his 300-member test group to spread the news. Without one bit of advertising, Amazon.com sold books not only in 50 states but also overseas. To Jeff's delight, his idea and web-site promised to be "something much bigger than we ever dared to hope."

Jeff knew that he could not just sit around and wait for his company to grow on its own. He wanted a constant updating of the site, always with customer convenience in mind. As he told one reporter, "Customer service—the nonglamorous parts of the business," was far more important than the website's appearance. He later compared Amazon.com's customer-friendly site to those of other e-commerce sites:

This six-year timeline of Amazon.com's history reflects the tremendous risks Jeff has taken, as well as the rewards his choices brought.

Jeff is often compared to Steve Jobs, above, founder and iCEO of Apple Computer. Unlike Steve, however, Jeff's efforts are more targeted toward providing his customers with new services rather than computer hardware and software.

"A lot of these companies that are coming online spend all their money and effort building a beautiful website and then they can't get the stuff to the customers."

In his early days in Internet business, Jeff was compared to two other famous computer figures: Steve Jobs of Apple Computer and Bill Gates of Microsoft. All three men have displayed extreme vision and talent in developing computers or computer services. However, Jeff differs from the other two men. First, while the other two invented the hardware and software that made personal computing popular, Jeff took advantage of their inventions to make a new service possible. Second, while Jobs and Gates have reputations as moody intellectual types, Jeff has an easy-going personality. His legendary laugh sounds often and long. Unlike many executives, he seems to enjoy interacting with his employees. The coldest journalists have warmed to his infectious good humor. When a great gale of laughter moves down the hall of his Seattle office, his employees know that the boss has arrived.

But Jeff never considered his work a laughing matter. He knew from the beginning that only continued dedication to his vision would keep the company alive. As his online business matured, he would face many critics predicting Amazon.com would fail.

4

CHOOSE, CLICK, CHECK OUT

Jeff showed no surprise when those critical of his business predicted its failure. Even though Yahoo, an Internet directory, listed Amazon.com for one year on its "What's Cool Page," Jeff's venture was the new kid on the block. It had to compete with booksellers, such as Barnes & Noble and the Borders Group, which had been around for a while. Those stores had steady customers and lots of books to sell.

For a year or so, those traditional bookstores didn't even notice the newly formed online bookseller. Then in 1996 the *Wall Street Journal*, a widely-read business newspaper, put a story about the company on its front page. Suddenly, the well-known book businesses took notice of the young upstart. Book stores and distributors had yet to go online, and many began to wonder whether they should consider doing so.

More importantly, the story caught the attention of a huge new group of possible customers. Still, business experts scoffed at the idea that Amazon.com could compete with the better-known bookstores. One executive

Famous among his employees for his easy-going manner and sense of humor, Jeff insists that the success of Internet companies depends on customer service. His "choose, click, and check out" ordering method is designed with those customers in mind.

even called it "Amazon.toast," expecting it to be an immediate failure. However, it proved anything but a failure as the number of happy customers grew. Suddenly, people wanted to own a part of this successful business.

Once again, experts were doubtful. After all, older businesses had profits, with money left over after paying their bills. Amazon.com had no profits in its first, second, third, fourth, and even its fifth year. Jeff joked about that, saying, "Most people don't know this, but actually we were profitable very early on—for about an hour in 1995."

Unlike many company executives, Jeff did not distribute Amazon.com's earning to its stock holders. Instead, he used the money to improve customer service and product selection. One of those improvements included a website that was easier for customers to use. A second improvement focused on offering new products. While Amazon at first sold only books, within a few years it offered other goods to its shoppers. These improvements only encouraged more people to invest in the company.

When Amazon.com's stock first went on sale to the public in 1997, one share cost less than $20. That one share would later grow to be worth in excess of $200, or more than 10 times the original investment. Of course, not everyone would make that kind of money from their Amazon.com stock. As with any stock, owners would have to decide when to sell their investments. Stock prices change, going higher or lower depending on how many people want to buy them on any specific day. But regardless of its price, stock sales of Amazon.com continued to boom.

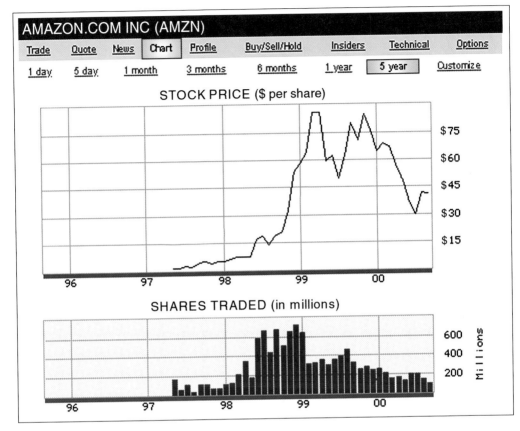

The upper chart shows the changing cost per share for Amazon.com's stock, and the lower chart shows the number of shares traded measured in millions-per-month, since the company's inception. Some critics express concern that the company has yet to show a profit. But instead of taking profits, Jeff chooses to use earnings to improve customer service.

Experts in stocks found it puzzling that so many people were willing to buy stock in a company that showed no profits. That had not happened in the past with "brick and mortar" companies. However, they would see it happen more and more with new Internet companies. Investors seemed willing to wait for the company to make profits. They chose to invest in the future.

Jeff Bezos really appreciated his investors. What's more, he understood his need for happy customers too; they were what really made his company valuable. He knew that if he stopped focusing on improvement, he could bring disaster to his company. The results of his hard work, his constant push to improve his business through customer service, and his business's value could disappear overnight. He believed that in order to "build something important and lasting," he had to continue to put the money back in the company and to operate a high-risk business.

Never asking others to do what he himself would not do, Jeff purchased many shares of his own business. He and MacKenzie would eventually own almost half of the company. He said, "We've been totally straightforward with everybody from the beginning that that's our strategy, and a lot of people believe in our strategy and some people don't. Reasonable people could disagree." Ultimately, Jeff's actions would make him a multimillionaire. But before that day arrived, much hard work lay ahead.

Jeff knew that he had to continue to upgrade and perfect his website. He put his computer programmers to work developing the most customer-friendly website to be found. They met and surpassed the challenge, setting up the now-famous one-click method of online shopping. Customers had only to find a book they wanted, use a computer mouse to click on their selection, and the computer would record their choice. It also accepted payment by credit card or agreed to bill the customer. Then it collected information that allowed home delivery. Each of those stages of purchase required very simple actions on the customers' part.

For example, customers needed to be able to find a book easily. Some customers came to the site already knowing the name of their favorite book. After clicking on the choice labeled "Title" from several choices offered, they could type in the book's name. Immediately the book's title would appear on the screen with the book's price. Eventually, as the site added improvements, shoppers could view pictures of many of the books' covers.

Should customers simply want to buy any book by a favorite author, they needed only to choose "Author." By typing in the name Orson Scott Card, for instance, readers could view a list of science-fiction titles by that author. Again, they simply clicked on the title of choice. Even if some customers had neither title nor author in mind, a book on a favorite subject could be located. All the customers needed to do was type in that subject. Whether they wanted to read about baseball or movies, rap music or Leonardo DiCaprio, the titles of any books about the subject would appear.

After customers made their selections, the books could be added to their basket. Just as in a typical grocery store, Amazon shoppers could fill up a cart. A picture of a shopping cart appeared at the top of the website's pages. The use of this familiar object made the shoppers feel more relaxed about an online shopping experience. After all, for many people, Amazon.com was the first e-store they had ever visited.

Another comfort phrase appeared following an item's selection. The web page asked whether it was time to proceed to "check out." Again, shoppers would be familiar with the idea of checking out with their purchases; they did it often in stores. At check out, customers provided a credit card number or other payment information. Next, they would give a mailing address. Finally, the customers received a special order number that helped identify the purchase later, should it not arrive when promised. For questions such as "Why hasn't my order been shipped to me?" customers could, with another click, "talk" to Amazon's customer service.

Jeff's unwavering focus on service acted as a challenge to other e-businesses. Just when customers learned how to use and enjoy one service, Jeff offered another. Eventually, those who had read books sold by Amazon could share their thoughts about the books with others. Jeff allowed readers to write and post their reviews on the web pages for individual books. That helped other people decide whether they might like to purchase the book. Authors were also invited to make comments about their own books.

Amazon even invited customers to suggest possible titles for books to be written by their favorite authors. For instance, mystery writer Sue Grafton moved through the alphabet with her mystery titles. The first in her series was named *A Is for Alibi*. This was followed by *B Is for Burglar*. By the time Amazon customers began their discussion, she had written *M Is for Murder*. Readers of her mysteries debated with one another about the name of her next book. Titles such as *N Is for Nuts* and *N Is for Nausea* were suggested.

Very quickly, Amazon became something more than just a place to buy a book. Still, it had not offered anything that traditional bookstores could not offer—not, that is, until Jeff began to think about those displays that stand in the fronts of such stores.

In most instances, when people walk into bookstores, they notice special displays at the

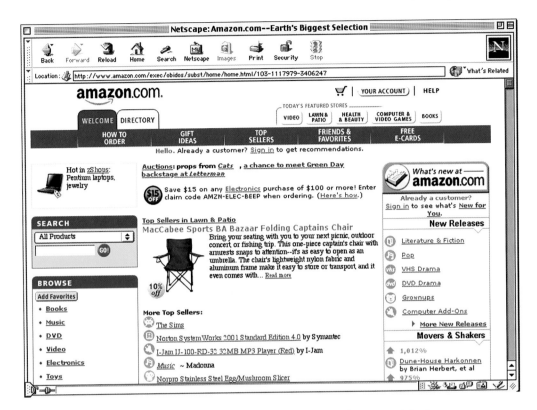

front of the store. Perhaps a life-size cardboard figure of one of the characters from the *Star Wars* series stands beside a table stacked with the book versions of those stories. Another table might hold all of the latest romance books. These catch the attention of readers who especially liked that type of book. Jeff knew that he could add pictures to the website, but they might appeal to only a select group of readers, as the store displays did. He wanted to go a step beyond that approach.

Jeff told his computer programmers that he wanted to help each individual reader choose books that they would like. Suddenly, Amazon offered a service that no regular store could duplicate. The site kept records of each customer's purchase. Then it offered customers

As this homepage from Amazon.com's ever-changing website shows, Jeff constantly offers customers new services to choose from.

the chance to view books covering the same subject when they returned to the website. The site could recognize customers' computers when the customer visited Amazon.

For example, if John Smith had purchased the book *The Adventures of Tom Sawyer* by American author Mark Twain, the next time he visited, he would see a message on the website that read, "Hello, John Smith. We have recommendations for you." The site might suggest the book *The Adventures of Huckleberry Finn*, another of Mark Twain's classics. Later, when Amazon offered products in addition to books, the choices increased to music, DVDs, and more.

Another banner on the page read "New for You." Such ideas could be credited to Jeff's tireless devotion to his vision of doing something that had never been done before. A sentence on thermal cups that he mailed out as a gift to many of his customers captured that idea. The quotation, written by a famous French writer named André Gide, read, "People cannot discover new lands until they have the courage to lose sight of the shore."

While Amazon proved a success in many ways, it never claimed to be perfect. What may have surprised some people has been its quick movement to admit and correct its errors. In 1998, some publishers studying the website claimed that other publishers had received better treatment. Amazon seemed to feature certain publishers' books more than it did those of others. Not only did the company admit the mistake, but it immediately went to work to be sure that it offered equal treatment to all publishers.

The company also acted quickly to correct

another mistake involving a country in Europe. In 1999, German authorities contacted Amazon about a book it had been shipping to their country. Titled *Mein Kampf*, the book had been written decades before by Adolf Hitler, the infamous leader of Germany from 1933 to 1945. German law clearly banned the German version of *Mein Kampf* from circulation, but it was not clear if the law also applied to the English versions that Amazon.com had been sending to German customers. Amazon immediately halted all mailings of the book to Germany. These actions gave people increased confidence in Amazon.com.

Jeff and Amazon have been mentioned along with Sam Walton, Wal-Mart's founder, and Robert Wood, known for helping Sears grow, as the 20th century's top marketing geniuses.

Sam Walton, from a small Arkansas town, opened his first tiny store in that small town and used a donkey out front to lure customers in. What amounted to a first-try failure did not discourage Walton. He had faith in his vision to create a store that would sell many products at lower prices than any other retailer. He later built Wal-Mart into the most successful, low-cost retail chain ever.

Walton had learned about vision from the earlier efforts of General Robert Wood. The general had directed construction on the Panama Canal and served as the U.S. Army's main supply officer in World War I. After studying both the changing population in the United States and the places where people were deciding to live, in 1919 he went to work for Montgomery Ward. At that time, Ward sold retail goods by catalog only. General Wood

Like Wal-Mart founder Sam Walton, shown here, Jeff has revolutionized the way many Americans shop for goods and services.

tried to convince his bosses that they needed to establish stores and make direct sales, taking advantage of the growing highway system that could bring people into stores. A Ward's executive didn't like the idea, and he fired the general. Wood wasn't out of a job for long, and he was soon hired by Sears Roebuck. Using his plan, Sears jumped from catalog sales to direct sales from stores. Before long, Sears became the world's top retailer.

Just like these two innovators, Jeff embraced new challenges. Unlike Wood and Walton, however, Jeff Bezos had to act quickly to shape his business in surroundings that changed every day. In 1998, Amazon was still years away from showing any profits. Many experts believed it would succeed because Jeff had found a great product for online shoppers. Books don't break during shipment or come in the wrong size. But what about all those other products Amazon.com would soon unveil? Could they enjoy the same popularity as books?

THE FUTURE
IS NOW

In June 1998, Jeff decided to add music CDs to Amazon's product list. The site offered a selection of music 10 times greater than what could be found in any music store. In addition to huge selection, it also offered huge savings. Prices were often almost half that charged in stores. Four months later, Amazon could call itself the biggest online music seller. By the end of 1998, the business had purchased two Internet companies that allowed it to enter Europe's electronic markets. It opened sites in the United Kingdom and Germany. Jeff Bezos's business was on the move.

In an interview in March 2000, Jeff spoke of the music-selling business. He said, "We're very grateful to all the customers that have chosen to shop at our music store. The main reason they shop at Amazon is because we put so much work into the music experience so people can quickly and easily discover what it is they're looking for—maybe even discover something brand new that they never would have found in any other way." When asked what kind of music and artists he liked to listen

Surrounded by fans and admirers, Jeff continues to believe that his success depends on the loyalty of his customers. His top priority is to make them happy.

to, Jeff mentioned Sarah McLachlan, the Indigo Girls, and Amanda Green. He also likes listening to "quirky things," like the *Battlestar Galactica* theme song. Before closing the interview, he added, "I always love to thank our customers, because that's why we are what we are today."

Not only has Jeff made customers happy, his stock owners have also been happy. Two different times in 1998, Amazon enjoyed a three-for-one stock split. That meant that for every one share investors owned, two additional shares would automatically become theirs. At the same time, the price of one share of stock was divided by three. That way, people who felt they could not afford the stock when one share cost around $200.00, could buy it when that cost fell to about $70.00. As soon as the stock price lowered, massive amounts of the stock sold. That caused the price to go right back up again.

Eventually, Amazon stock staged three different such splits. That meant that a person who originally bought 100 shares of Amazon.com stock for less than $20 per share, could have ended up owning 2,700 shares worth more than $100 each. Clearly, Jeff's efforts had resulted in a significant financial success.

Naturally, Jeff felt pleased with his progress, but he retained his vision of growing ever bigger. He always kept in mind the fact that people, not computers, made his business run. One of the company's benefits is to allow employees to invest in Amazon.com stock at a low price. That has made many of them wealthy. One Amazon motto that all the employees learn and practice is "Work hard, have fun, and make history."

Most of Amazon.com's employees are in their 20s. All workers are allowed to dress comfortably for work. They can wear running shoes to complete the miles they have to walk up and down aisles, finding products ordered by customers.

The employees need those running shoes. In 1999 and 2000, Jeff made many more products available through Amazon. Customers could purchase videos and pet supplies, computer software and toys, electronics and DVDs, tools and hardware, even lawn and patio supplies. There seemed to be nothing that could not be found through Amazon. The site also could link visitors to another site with auctions on the Internet, where they could bid what they wanted to pay for many different items. The site suggested gift ideas, too, offering special wrapping and also links to free electronic cards. Jeff Bezos would not be caught napping while others in electronic business forged ahead.

Although Amazon is part of an entirely new business approach, Jeff still feels he can learn from history. At one meeting of Internet business executives in California, he stood on the stage waving a thick sheaf of papers. Those in the audience learned that the papers were a printout of hundreds of names. Each name represented a company that had existed in the 1920s when there was so much excitement about the relatively new invention known as the automobile, and most of the company names contained the word "car." Then Jeff pointed out that only a few of those companies still exist. Jeff made the comparison to present-day businesses that are anxious to add ".com" (dot-com) to their names just because it's something new. He does not want

Amazon to be on a similar list waved at an audience 100 years from now.

Throughout 1999 and 2000, Jeff began building six enormous warehouses in different parts of the country. He chose their locations carefully in states that charge little or no state taxes. Together, they cost $200 million and can hold endless items. They will allow Jeff's employees to deliver large varieties of goods directly to the customer very quickly—usually in one or two days. In one warehouse, the walls are white and the dozens of shelves shine fluorescent yellow. Throughout the space, banners hang from the walls. As big as billboards, the banners help remind the employees of the things that Jeff considers important. One reads, "Our vision is the world's most customer-centric company," meaning Amazon must always keeps the satisfaction of its customers at the center of all its actions.

The business's never-ending personal attention to its customers continues to emphasize this philosophy. In one of its developments during 2000, Amazon.com offered to include customers in what it calls "Purchase Circles." The site describes these circles as "highly specialized bestseller lists" based on anonymous data gathered from orders sent to particular postal ZIP Codes. Using specialized formulas, Amazon.com determines items that are more popular in specific cities, workplaces, and colleges and universities than with the general population. Through the lists, customers can discover what products people in their hometown, at their workplace, or attending the school they went to are buying. Amazon has also provided a way for companies to have their Purchase Circle lists removed.

Even the business experts who had criticized Jeff's reinvestment in his company may soon find nothing to criticize. In 2000, Jeff predicted that Amazon would show a profit in the year 2001. Although Amazon's stock price moved wildly up and down along with other Internet companies' stocks in 2000, it maintained a relatively high price. Those who know about the stock market predict that many of the Internet companies' stocks popular in previous years may disappear after the market settles

This new Amazon.com warehouse facility located in Campbellsville, Kentucky, is one of six new warehouses that were built during 1999 and 2000. Scores of job seekers lined up to apply for employment when it first opened.

Dressed in chef's attire, Jeff shows his cooking products to home-management guru Martha Stewart during the launch of Amazon Kitchen. Never satisfied with what he's already accomplished, Jeff realizes that the future of his business depends on his constantly making new decisions.

down. Amazon is not among those companies. While no one can predict with complete accuracy how the price of a stock might change, Amazon's continued popularity over a five-year span shows it has a lot of support.

Jeff's personal life has also changed. Five years after founding his company, he and MacKenzie moved from their small apartment into a big house north of Seattle. They had their first child, a son, in March 2000, and the future looks bright for the young family.

Jeff understands that the future could hold some surprises, either good or bad. The quick changes in the stock market could hurt Amazon. However, with more than one billion dollars in the company account, his business will be protected for a time even with constant stock price changes. Another threat could be the very action that Jeff thought would improve Amazon: adding more products. Some of the critics of this move say that Amazon needs to specialize in one or two areas in order to be able to offer top-notch service.

But for the time being, those most important to Jeff's business—the customers—continue to show their support. They like Amazon's products and its attention to their needs, and they also seem to approve of Jeff's pioneering spirit. Jeff Bezos has achieved his vision, and that's an American success story that anyone can enjoy.

CHRONOLOGY

1964	Jeffrey Preston born on January 12 in New Mexico.
1968	Mother, Jackie Gise, marries Miguel "Mike" Bezos, who later adopts Jeff.
1986	Graduates from Princeton University with highest honors; takes first job with Fitel.
1988	Hired by Banker's Trust.
1990	Hired by D. E. Shaw.
1992	Becomes D. E. Shaw's youngest senior vice president.
1993	Marries MacKenzie.
1994	Decides to take advantage of the rapidly growing Internet; moves to Seattle to create a website to sell books.
1995	Amazon.com opens for public use in July.
1996	Article about Amazon.com in *The Wall Street Journal* boosts its growing popularity; Jeff patents one-click technology.
1997	Price of Amazon.com stock skyrockets.
1998	Amazon.com adds music to its sales and opens sites in the United Kingdom and Germany.
1999	Dozens more products added to Amazon.com; Jeff selected *Time* magazine's Person of the Year; relocates to a large house in Seattle suburb; begins to erect enormous warehouses in various locations in the United States.
2000	Predicts that Amazon.com will make a profit in 2001; son born in March.

FURTHER READING

Chambers, Elnora. *The Kid-Friendly Computer Book.* Menlo Park, Calif.: Monday Morning Books, 1997.

Gralla, Preston. *Online Kids: A Young Surfer's Guide to Cyberspace.* New York: John Wiley & Sons, 1996.

Hunter, Jennifer. "Amazon's Kingpin." *Maclean's,* June 21, 1999.

Martin, Michael H. "The Next Big Thing: A Bookstore?" *Fortune,* December 9, 1996.

Martinez, Yleana. "Lord of the Jungle." *Hispanic,* January 1999.

Quittner, Joseph. "1999 Person of the Year: Jeffery P. Bezos." *Time,* December 27, 1999.

Wolff, Michael. *Kids Rule the Net: The Only Guide to the Internet: Your Personal Net.* New York: Wolff New Media, 1996.

INDEX

ABOUT THE AUTHOR

VIRGINIA BRACKETT holds a Ph.D. in English and teaches at Triton College in River Grove, Illinois, near Chicago. Her published books include *Elizabeth Cary: Writer of Conscience* and *Classic Love and Romance Literature*. Her third book, *Early Women Writers: Voices from the Margin*, will be published in 2001. Her articles and stories have appeared in numerous magazines, including *Children's Digest*, *Turtle*, *Junior Trails*, *Living with Teenagers*, and *Children's Writer*.